WILDPLASSEN

dove / Chris Kirubi

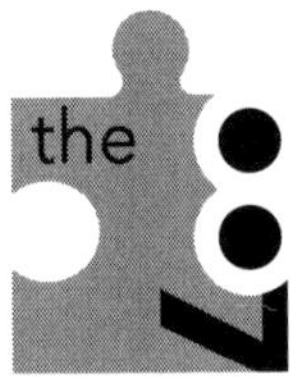

Published 2024 by the87press

The 87 Press LTD

87 Stonecot Hill

Sutton

Surrey

SM3 9HJ

www.the87press.co.uk

ISBN: 978-1-0686446-0-3

Printed and bound by CPI Group (UK) Ltd, Croydon, CR0 4YY

Cover image © 'Tolled', 2023, Shenece Oretha

Design: Stanislava Stoilova [www.sdesign.graphics]

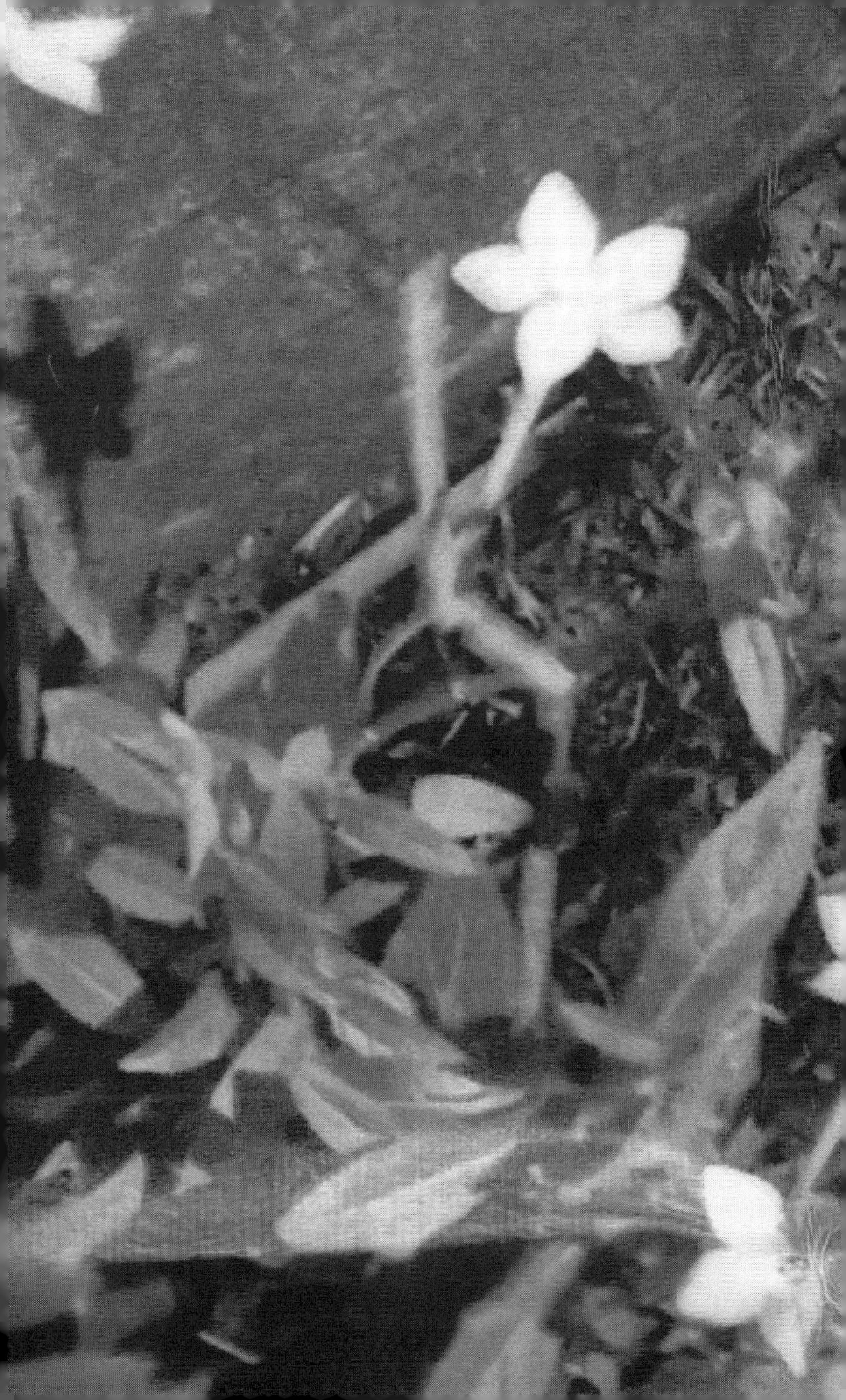

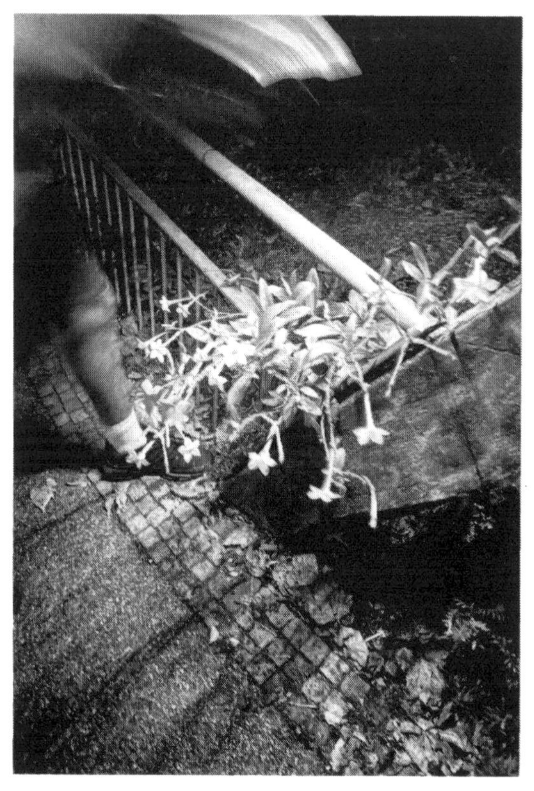

(lying

together   *had my*   love   true),

coming

i was a kid   so good
at calling the cops on myself
now i don't   want to state
who i am   & i   will not say my name
i don't want   a status   the states
two blue checks   checking up on me   (& you
can check the cctv)
it's time for me to loiter   as the colour
of soil   *i need*   to walk
very slowly   too slow   to be useful
to be followed   *to flower*   shadowed
wondered—,

bitten from my husk   held at
threshpoint   where the sill unwinds
& turns the lathe of my escaping
trample me   into the floor
of the american sugars
that refined my tongue   licking
the torn ceiling of europe
smirking   insurmountable
steel   glass   false light   false
winking cameras   waving air
charms   buzzes   hums   ticks
snorts   delineates

every shaking thought   each claim
to lucidity   so sly this land
sprinting to its decline   fighting
its own mind   & mine   tired
doubting   irresponsible   irreparable
unresponsive   individual
london's revolving eye   detached
from its own doom   sparkling against
the perfect detail   of birds   of morning
the capital makes the sun   ~~rise~~

o small thing of myself
at the centre of every sky
o loose illusion   *o* pale pupil
leaking broken systems
into the sea   *o* cry
of american babies
accessing air   gathering fathers
grazing mirrored minerals
swallowing miles of smoke
hurtling straight for the cameras

contractions   contracts   contradictions
pricked by this thistlefingered island
beating a rhythmless language
against shards of uncontrolled growth
biospheric biting at the suns
unproductive glory
jealous clutching fingers
tighten against the pressure
digging—…   finding—…   & there i am—,

implied in airspace   an infant   staring
out at the sky's name   of fuel
toothless tonguemonger   complicit
incomplete   another story
of the eye   going round & round
a status   updated   a natureless flower
a small thing   burning through clouds
a light feeling   burning up
making kids   of us all

—,& what of the licked edge
of dreaming   of the work of dawdling
unoccupied   ungrafted
from the grid
of these doubts   insatiable
accelerating

                     animate depths
  , breath   unsustainable
    swollen

              eye   & ear
                         -ly errors

         ,—?

(~~life—!~~
cannot be argued
inflicted or   alleviated
a smoke   a
-fraid   of its own
directness   , the field
of its own
                    distortions
,—but i can
       be punctuated
by fear by f
          -light,   ),

pattern
  & power   just
-ifications
in the frame
      -work
&—*!*,(
) i—*!*   unreal
  -istic   in
         -sistent
  insolent & in
          -subordinate
fffff
        -rustrate
           -d   —*!*
  . spec   -ulate
        hope
         -lessly late
            -nt

, i know use
    noise
        , *no—!*   (—&, on time
            i know   very little)
                ow—!   , little time   keep
    -ing this high
                        -ly   activ
        -ated   *k*
                            -otic
state ~~*pro*~~

            con

                    -ductive

sometimes on the street i pass
a wanderer   who swings
sweetshaped   as an apple
unfollowed fellow feeler
in a cloud of pocket music
the voices of those
in the past   dreaming of
thin papers   the rolling hills
of burgess park always

the gentle vibrations
cans in a plastic bag
loyal   to the slow pace
low life   let the breeze
keep the time   keep
sleeping
dissolute accomplices
diffuse explanations
just a jaywalk away…… ,

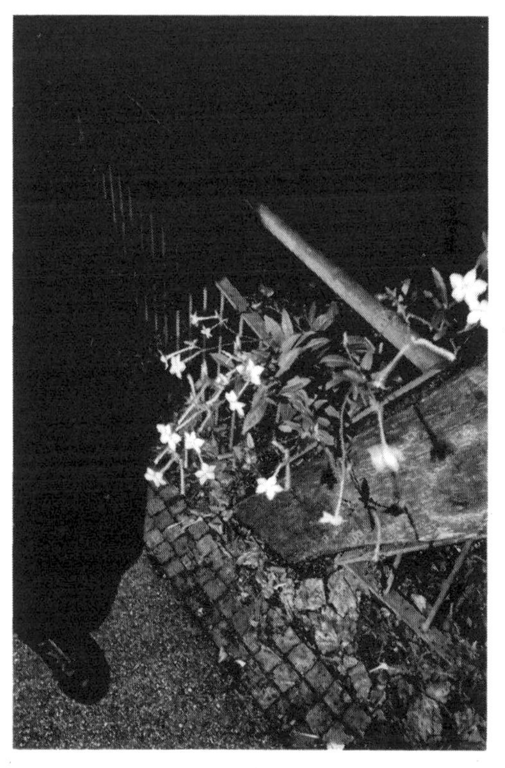

, *where*   (the swelling lake
            in your t-shirt

                        rehearses the moonlight),

there's roadworks now,
and scaffolding
when last time i walked this way

it was just massive puddles
all pressed together, weatherless
and hopeless this time

of cop, politician, celebrity or boss,
torsos and tunnels of their most
swollen extortions

to start the repair of the swell
and the swell of the weather
to see

contractual misleadings at the unsigned grid
whose sharp sheath becomes
the teethed concern   *can you please send me*

some sort of undeserved position
at which i owe the aching hours
that cumulate my life?

the other night was upsetting.
ideas were held above

the station of our heads,
like sweating and blinking stars

in undulating relief.
the sealed vision of citizens

is an access point, sudden
and hurtling towards the lure

of a great softening.
porous and shrinking camera

nakedly brandishing the light
of the common betrayal,

fingering its white device. the citizens
swarm toward their promise,

imagining the unfolding hiss
of a bit of ink.

like gel it fades in the disarming light,
silicone based, exacting ownership.

cloys to learn, finally, its speech
compressed against wet graphics

secreted by puddles
at pavements dull edge.

there is no reprieve from the sound
of the rattling fountain.

burr through room corners,
mischief toned gone birdedged, re-
peal   but sing birdsense —*!*

jamais plus *!*   SEMBÈNE sees   what pays le pays   how to say   paid to the tune of the (BLANK) property management company   (in these my (BLANK) hours)   petty cash   and petit lease   tout lisse   loose   lost   lui   ça *!*   *c'est pays !* under management of BLANC hands now and at the hour of their petty theft   their petty death   at the hand of their petits morts   nos petits mots (jamais plus   *!*) the HUSH of these hours   no more than a (BLANK) word   the white world no more (than this (   ))   beginning and ending with capital   hush money   paid hands   have the DIRT   de tes espoirs (despair)   repetez-vous   (no more *!*)

in the middle of UHURU   the mud of reign   in the midst of the mire   the militant milieu   the monetary fund   the mondiale   (the tout-monde(too much(too many)))   too little few   fell   dry   dirt   returns   as tax   an axe   (fill in the (   ) of the annexe international)(the white knack of the building)   (the BLANC of the *i*)   FEW pupil   or less   BLANK eyeing the moins of the money   this means (there is (no more *!*) they say)   comment dit-on   NEVER again (?)   this dust   ((disgust)   that razed (the sun) without rising)   it is to IMMURE to be nation   nascent immaturity the MATTER of these walls   their sphere   SPHÉRIQUE (to be (BLANK) attached to air) self means to see in obscurity   to see LE/LA   VOILE   NOIR(E)   le vol   across the dark (c) O SEA / OCEAN   (O STRONG is the FORT *!*)

the implications of placing a bus stop here
seem to disperse whatever happened in the theatre,
it might have just been the hang of his wet t-shirt
against the swelling of what we were that ignited
the grin between his eyes. men haunt this place.
police gaze, desiring and alert. i don't know though,
i wasn't there, i couldn't get a ticket. coils of hair
linger on the ground. crumbs, dandelions. footsteps
rhythms of sunlight stain the arms
of these weatherstroked rooms.
the swiping of the inside seams of his trousers
makes his voice drop. happy heaving is all carried off now,
carried to where the birds hunt amongst the windows
for materials with which they might build their nests.
but the heaving becomes brittle, sallow and strange.
the slim book looks back at me through barely recognisable
blossomings of corporate sweat forming on the window.
unbalanced thoughts suddenly possible
in the unfolding stupor, the stewing magic that clouds
the jagged spark. i crawl against the wet grey glass,
cracking it in a carpeted, recorded fever.

huddled around the table is every single person
that had anything to do with the decision,
the spreading that measures up to our historical imaging.
the decision deepens, there is no reason to defend it now.
it is bound to straddle and express what the building
was designed to contain. no lilting can enjoy these
swerving aggregations, the gesturing that the graphs
clearly show as being inadvertently enshrined. still,
i wonder who was there to take the image.
what the consequences of their humming might mean

for the images circulation. was the flight noticed?
the faculty will fine anyone with any desire to locate
the complaints that course gravel day and night, until
all the skips fill up with tiny birds and nothing
rises from the serenity of the beeping.

slow mood tiring in the click of the child of the logo. it is
the fact of their brokenness that stands outside, crossing the
bridge as bunting announces the arms circumference, as seen
as the river and so soon in the leatherless fold craving the
short straight light. something to let out in the puff of its
gesture.

it is the fact of their brokenness that scares me, sitting like
cold and colourless rain on the tarmac. the quality of this
space is available, and acrylic and always straining alongside
the doubt's slick touch, the ridiculous mixing of polish is
frightening to the top of whatever the lungs momentarily
contain.

i've been strummed in the end, although i have to say that
when i first met you, you seemed sealed off and quiet like
the ideal type of place that i would go to have some food
and say that i'd be ready to receive the menu now.

a salad spills in the street; wing and heart, sauces.
the bus barely avoids it. its mistake spreads all over
the sidewalk. it pricks and prods, breaking
the information that burns away at the allegiances
that hold these boroughs together. the discovery
weighing down the negative likeness of beet sugar

clinging to the colonial mind as it pounds against the dry
illuminations of the dirt. my features shadows chase
amplified confinement. they are stuck here, and with them
the frightened alphabet that they have drawn all over
my forehead in permanent markers. the colour bleeds
right through the brick, and its tertiary reversal scrapes

and laughs, fingering the pages of its moisturising factors,
crisp, white and hydrophobic, the result of being unable
to identify the proliferating nature of gendered processes.
even amongst friends, the shine of a coin settles.
the messaging passes from cup to cup until the rawness
of all our strumming leaves us in drifting, hollow shade.

it was too late by the time we realised what their rivers
were made of. the strumming would warp the bridge
as they moved from room to room, leaving behind them
great piles of broken furniture. the tapping is distorted
by this tension, following the wiring right through the wall.
its claimants overdue. i can no longer read their arrival.

and they happened in front of the clouds that wouldn't stop
forming beneath my eyes. it is not possible to know
how to dress for this weather. that window is more
glimpse than glimmer, really. reappearing. i no longer
want to live a disciplined life. and surely there must be
something else in the lens than refusing to focus
the gift of what has already been given to the sullen faces
against the window. the forever of that something pressing
against the velocity of the gap opening between us. a vector
that captures our conversations as they move
from the tired thoughts of our complicated clambering.
subtle grief converts and the map narrows again, as if
to encourage the recovery of all dreams. perhaps dreams
were the aggressors we'd heard. it is only on waking
that reassurance captures the blame of half-veiled hanging,
as if it were veiling, or halving, that terrified us
in the first place.

night is chased by a brushing of hourly fingertips,
i was glad that you turned up. i should not have been left
alone in this state with my dreams, fleeting
and unconcerned by the laughter of our steps down the corridor.
no cooing of the throat anymore, no subdued anxiety,
just the new river shuttling against my understanding
of this place and its residual elimination of what
cannot be found without walking into the water, constantly
making its flow from sweat, no longer looking through glass
but grasping what the cobalt gloss refuses.
you could hear the emboldening of our improvisations
the other night, the noticing of our flesh. coagulation
is the wrong word since the move is one of possession
and frequencies that stretch across the corpus of the group.

do you remember when we lived next to the daylight
of the overground platform, and only certain things
could happen in that room
where the window faced people waiting for the train?

secondje

> *dat kan niet*
> *da'k hier ben gewoon*
> *om gelukkig te worden*

second movement

> ~~*een dwang*~~
> *dat ik niet nodig heb*
> *die niet van mij is*

fear arpeggaic. the sounds they must have heard,
believing it to be descent & macropolitic's fine mist
particles of their damp colour. buzzing flutter
around the work's shivering branding
waiting for the day that i

> , everything, will not be
> a constraint against the loss
> , that could waste my life.

> sacrifice scale tremble at the first measure
> of melodic tool without the phrase to listen
> or leap to shaping upper register
> and risk the language that flattened noses,
> good at endings.

> shores of zone 1's very,
> very personal, shattered
> attentions

> a study that will tell us
> whether it's safe to go back,
> and for who.

> this section in compound time for some reason,
> just one of these thoughts at a time, and they are very,

very sorry but i cannot be kept behind that same glass
half-voiced insult of money, the scale that coiled hair
to mineral light rendering passive where   zimbacca,
                                               bédouin,
                                            & péret
                              could invent the world

by borrowing it from the collection / of theirs a bit
more time—, smearing the inverted passage
fingernail breaks the semibreve but dots the semiquaver
notation of these the men defend forever   , i cannot
                                                   just be here
                                                   to be happy,

                         a constraint
                         that i do not need / i count out
                         the rest out of the rests / i learn
to tremble (& *i fear*

          all images) / throw

hard ballot right into shrieking ballot box sirens, my personality
run out of options cannot defend anymore choices,
there is only one left

and it is not for a life too big to maintain / sublet
decimation
antiphonal / why
                         should its use pass through me,
                         through what

                         i have seen, the sounds
                         i must have heard
                         in freakish
                                   descant

sorry bramble

prophetic i mean
   sorry no   pathetic no   uprooted
ash is smoke   //snow   off-peak
   & at the edge of buildings   burn
corrodes their concrete glass
   sorry city   sorry steel no
steal no money sorry i think money
as white is now across sorriest city
     moniest footsteps i mean
  as i steal across the city   it casts its net
   the big smoke
    no smile it cracks a smile   no wait
a big joke   isn't this all
 a little silly   sorry a little citizen   no a little
dizzy   a bit choked   a bit of a dream
    all this pollution   sorry this
   potential   no it's poison   a bit
of moneyish time   spending our
    hard times i guess   the best guess
(sorry*!!*)

floor board   boring it's   a prophet
  or a promise sorry   the offer   in the
dark   sorry park   the dark makes the park
  sorry   sorrier   //snowier   alpine no
   i pine   no opening   //no
i mean snow *!!* no i said yes sorry *!!*
      bulging burgess   bramble bushes *!!*
  there //'s no city   now   no there
   right there *!!*   circle back   back
turn sorry no   you have to earn it
   what if i can only earn it *!!*   sorry i'm afraid

       scared   & sorry   &//snowy
s//no -ish   no -esque   no adjacent
  is that rain —?   the biggest no
   the sorriest   sorrying prophecy
sorry no profiting no   positing   ye
  -s//no   i don't know !!
    please   (please)//s//now!!   burn
away the roof   it's gunna be flats anyway
  the safest place   to steal   in the dark   away
no   anyway it's gunna be flats   it'll all go
  fast no
                    sorryyyyyyyy !!
  they already sold them   stole them
i mean caught them   they already cast
  their net   their characters   sorry
sorrier   and sorriest   and the //snow of course
  i mean they know   of course they know
            they know now already
who's coming & who's going
   who's got to go & sorry   some of us
have just got to go   & how can we stay
  really it's too dark   the dark is sorry (sorry)
    sorry it's dark //snow (ash)   (dark)
as a wish   of ash   ash the earth
//so   nothing   sorry //sow nothing   no
grow nothing can reap   no so nothing reaps
  what nothing grows   sorry sows
    look   it's hard to control sorry   imagine
        the growth !!   the healing the snare
  no care sorry   the self-snare   see —?
    some of us !!   really have got to
//snow

to flickering closeup of flowers
where frenzy and romance
touch each other
appearing in momentary flight
of quick visual assonance

pink from observation
taking possession of air
aligning final diagrammatic
notes of sunlight, falling flat
against the need to foresee
the circumstances

yet now (rented)

but we are repurpose
comb and sweep and un
-sensed in that direction

falling into and out of
pages of held hands failed
strategies of being good

property disputes over
identifications with
all we have no desire

to keep one day to step
slip sneak i'd love toward
this and you too

to share the path with a small bird, slim glass
of water that someone has had while fretting
over having something to go to every week.

night tube trades in one kind of discomfort
for another, making noise to get home,
if it could beat the promise of its own image.

smudged & grounded
  shadows of clouds
or is it the ground that is
  smudged into lands

mapping passions
  or passage   infinite
-simal unfinished in
  -undated time

where there is love
  there is also distance in
-timate times love times
  also this dust which is

time   across & through
  & at the same time
aligning the eye to the
  level of the horizon

which has no equal
  separated now from what
we can never be   (gulls
  chase what i cannot see

or search for   stated
  stayed as duration)   dreaming
for the sun to change
  everything

minutes

that look and easier things will summer
at the favourite opening to slant at the touch
at the sprawling core of the small held
in and around our full hands, sighing love
of doubt. roll through the minutes
with matter of sleeps wild enfolding
of a few more of these with you.
clockstruck waste where we are hidden
attempting this afternoons wrong notes
and the failure of privacy to leave a mark
on our unused whistling
and unwillingness to project.

barely a bow on the sky to dream with.
cloudless and cupped to the pulling of my strings,
to the imprecision of late music.

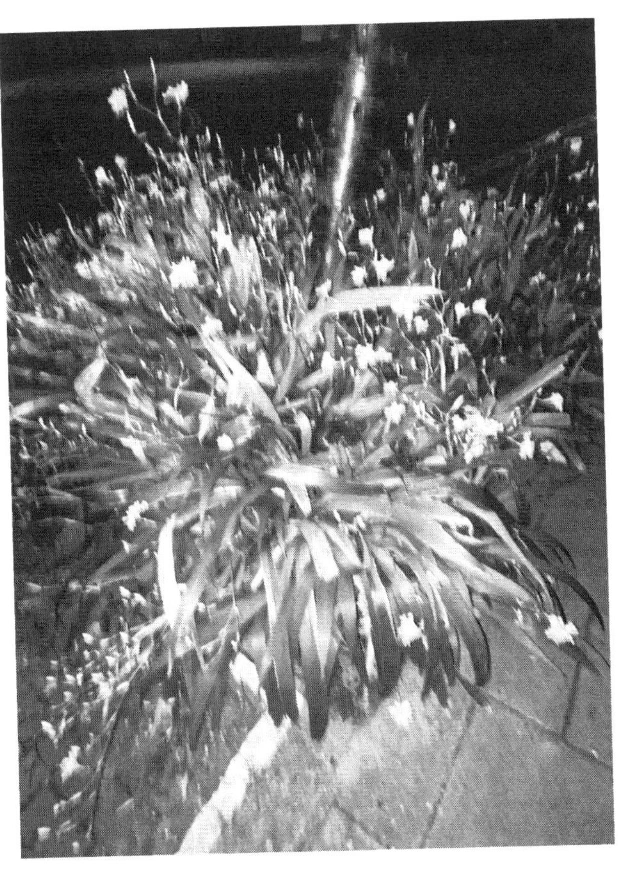

, & *(all over)* pissshakes

continuous   *miswandering—*

At breakfast the boiler broke again. The system did not allow for effective communication between technicians, and so each day a new one came. She woke her sister up. Small bird hopped, hopping again through what had become very old in her sisters room. A whole day of this certificate on the fridge with the wrong information on it. It had not been checked properly. Her sister shook her curls from her sleep, someone had built her bedroom around a boiler at eight thirty in the morning. She left the small bird to the expressions of her folklore and washed the bowl in cold water. British Gas argued with itself over the phone, powerless at this time. The date would not change.

She closed the window trying to quiet the buzzing outside. They were trying to take the sycamore down, things were not as they should be. The tree brought the hovering woodpeckers to the morning, the morning brought Friary Road to its ears, pressed lightly to what shifted in the cold. It could not be changed in disagreement, nor could it sit in reason, the tinkering of its cultured effects. Tale of falling, tall click of felling, tall voice of air over the road. It must be the garden's silence, someone must have hired it.

She faced the theatre of these things, their ability to measure her, the front door. She sat and blew the bug from the window before she closed it. She was not ready to text her friend back. Touched, tidied slowly. Twitter. Yesterday trembled again in drifting thrill of the small bird.

The night before she sat with her friend. It might take days to bring this tree down, and the days would wake her. Bad posture's terrific fugue, she shifted in the wooden chair behind the pianist. She folded her arms in the queue outside and glanced at the window. She had arrived early. There had been no hot water for three days, and no technician could get hold of the right parts to fix the boiler. Winglimbed blue cyphers occupied the form to verify the status of things. Their visit, and the advice. She had arrived before her friend who texted and asked if she would save a seat. The window swelled with the audience's arrival, their notes warmed the silence into retreat. She sat very close to the piano stool. Very close to the white couple beside her who smiled. Her friend arrived as the lighting changed and their chatter clicked and fluttered.

The improviser's hand rattled the calabash, the room. Rhythms. Her voice opening the texture of intentions, the sound of her friends questions as they drank, listening. It was nothing to wonder at their time together.

The tea was still. She needed to text her landlady who had a way with them. It was the only way to get British Gas to come in and out of the house all day with the right parts found, at last, on Old Kent road. The scent of her sister's cold shower as she said goodbye. The tree surgeon's bright ropes in the tree.

It was in the can of Coke, hiding in the offer. A look from another girl, warm, who recognised what she could tell. She told many times who she was in the living room, but could never explain. What time had it been when they all laughed again? The white curtains no longer kept the sunlight out.

"Bitch I can tell!", so she told, and shared and passed the little plate, and would leave all her decisions for tomorrow. The room of these people heightened, she was not the only girl among strangers. Although, again a girl. Passed out in a taxi. The exasperated driver paced up and down Paral·lel, the night wouldn't end. Police arrived and their fingers squeezed the tendons behind the girl's ear. She was in the car and both doors were blocked by Police. They had called Emergency Services, but she shouldn't have been there at all. Two pills would have done it, but some don't realise what they conceal in the offer.

It was in the national park. She was still wearing her friends clothes. The cat was asleep on the floor, and her friend was waiting for her at the river. She wasn't ready to go, this was the only decision she had made that day after the flight and then the train. The dreaming cat and the hot stone steps. The event fell further into the distance despite its crowded amplification. She wouldn't have been the only girl there, but she wouldn't be there at all. She climbed around, and texted her friend back.

"I've been trying to reach you for like six weeks". She pulled her curls out of the drain, her fingers went in to the knuckle. She was another, blurring through the endeavour of the streets. She went there often, to look at the consequences of the city, its seeds scattered as windows. Different seeds, a sea marked by its setting.

She looked down, outfigured again by sun. She went to the Carrefour to find things to go with pasta. The sun stayed up in the living room, the conversations on the edge of the couch, on his knee, in the bedroom. The translations danced from one foot to another, they took another trip to the shop. The girl told her that she had moved from Venezuela, where her somewhere else had been. There was something there that she was not able to miss.

The door in question was in the bathroom, in the kitchen. It closed shakily as she entered. She could not sleep before dinner and left early, fingering her pages on the flight. They would not see her here if she stayed, although she had met them. She now understood the brief exchange and what was written on the sign. And her sister. She lay for a while, and reached out. Her lips parted before she could realise what the offer was. Flown through the plane's pages, she went to his flat around the corner. It wasn't far.

She could lay there. Not a sycamore, but a cedar. The sycamore was to come down later, they had got a letter from the new owners. Their characters. The inconvenience standing in their doorway. Her afternoon whispered over the black, plastic pepper grinder. Lemon. Rinsed capers.

There was no end to the expense of 2018, its dull expressions of form. They had put a massive Gymbox in at Elephant & Castle and there was no end to it. At one time its huge adjacent billboard read *THE NEW KING OF THE CASTLE.* And where to go from that growth? The expense changed the skyline. The street, it felt impossible to tell. She veered again into the ditch, the cost of her material failures. She had to buy a can of Coke to stay awake. And then back under the shower with him.

He left for work at 7am. There was another room. There would be another where she could patch things up with failed materials, although she couldn't see it anymore. She had lost sight of it. She couldn't sleep. She didn't sleep for a few days. People did not sleep during the day, and this was not lost on her. It curled up in her hands, almost blank. Veered, dully. Almost empty. She banged on the door, peered inside the jutting and white architecture. She looked up. She looked away. Did not go up the lift.

Tall and white, he kept falling into her and laughing in her face. Unsweet, if she swung on him. But he kept falling, trampling the fennel beneath the feet of her friends. She wouldn't be ashamed. It was better to water the plants at night.

47

She left her room behind, and didn't mind if things didn't get done. There were many doves, and some pigeons by the time she got back. Somewhat blue and soundless, the sky clear of its cedar trees. The flowers drew the eye to the opening of the property. She felt that she shouldn't be looking up at their window.

And Elephant & Castle would be a block against the sky, a volume of skied expense. She remembered the guy she hooked up with. He was staying in a flat somewhere behind LCC. He said he had been wanting a high street put in for ages. She wondered what he thought now, is this what someone would have wanted in 2014? It seemed to express something else, it seemed aimed at someone else's expression. That flat had been his cousin's. He was crashing there while he tried to find somewhere else in the area of that year. He didn't appear again when she opened Grindr. He may as well have been. Although it was no other time.

There was one time in her meaning-riddled drunkenness that had been. She had been through the scale of the apartments, and could barely think of walking through the time of their streets.

"Mec, je t'avais dis qu'on vois les gens drogués içi," her friend was looking for her again. A sharp turn of wandering. The distorted details of the skyline. An image that had more space in it than there should be from this perspective.

Like thistle, but touched the path where a bird had lost some of its feathers. She couldn't recognise the shapes of the leaves webbed closely with dust, the stirring of its wings. The clouds played along before opening out onto what organised the land and produced the cover of the thistle in the picture. More ground than upending sky, a red that belonged more to fall. It wasn't for her to share its pace, she would need to scatter its berries close to the ground and the planes over the view.

And watch things drift over the little pile of cities, the bee very close to her skin. The figures walked over the landscape contoured by the plastic bag that had been moulded into the texture of the road by its traffic. A building site was there, the quiet and sharp field of its potential. The developer's bright, unending day. The strong, vertical strokes. People have always walked among the trees. She took a picture of what was behind her.

That again and again became worth its steps. Became worth the again and again of its steps, whose worth became what it meant to set foot on something. On somewhere again. And foot became against the setting of itself, the feet that came again, against the setting of ourselves. Incessant heats idyllic phrase and again, it could be small. Worth the share of its resources. And who was to say what a path was or wasn't. Someone had built an unfinished stair among the breeze avoiding the roots unnamed nature, and leaving would cast its red shade over airspace. Cold and drying to her skin when she had been a child. An access whose meaning she could not escape. The suspense brought her outside relation, too close to the skin.

Already, the light was changing the time zone, the fluorescence of its seal, the smell of the milk under the foil.

"As she gets higher, you need to strengthen the ground. That left hand", in firmness. It told its story, and grasped what was between her. An unaccompanied, urgent evening before she would walk across Burgess park. She would have to choose, and the mess made her late. The smell of the film inside her. And watched what suddenly ended, her small wait. Caught in the hair that led up to her navel, its sunlit unsureness in intervals, overgrown. She had no idea where the energy would come from, so she closed.

People filmed each other in the sun. A generation of men sitting in the sun of their sound, amplified beneath the trees. The thudding thumbs up of the joggers. The collapsing thistle and the mistake of the sycamore. The melted talking. Another car alarming through the leaves.

The cloud of birds was false. One man called to another. She woke, and it woke her, loud enough to shake a tree from its place in the sky. The room was barely a bed, then a window. It would wake her. They liaised with the sound of their chainsaw, the point of their air turned metal, their squawking air.

And there beside her sleepshape, she hadn't realised the window had been left open. In the hospital, on the plane. Red, wine drunk tears. Their warm way of doing things. She continued to sit, to be promised as far as hands would go without weft. And what had been written there she hadn't read, and she would not be drawn to its reading, but in carbon observation.

A note. In her sleep someone had passed her a crumpled piece of yellow paper with something written on it. A sheet of foil flattened onto the road. She walked to Boots and it reflected the texture of the road back at her, the flat heat of the environment. The sound of the cat as she walked into her room trekking dry dirt through the house, the shape of the mouth at its opening, thwarted, like the air and its gaps.

She walked along the side of the road and travelled at a speed that was not her own across its surface, the grey curls of its skin. And knew it very poorly. The mirror reflecting the intersection. An alignment shown to be incapable of interacting, concealed in the composition's centre, turning its loop.

The conversation lingered in tears, holding her aunt's basket, bowing the sisal against itself. It made a sound like talking, like something unwoven as it was in the afternoon of that room.

The glass poured with the felling of the trees at the end of the road. Sensed by a gap between the letters of the birds. The leaves fled and the atmosphere rushed to fill in the blue contribution of the sky. To then sink into the bird lit sky. And then the picture took her against the bird lit sky. And then the somewhat sun shaken blue sank in that direction, and then in dizzying, sun shaken rain took the birds against the edge. The birds at the edge of the trees in the light of the room, its falling mirror edged with photographs taken by windows. Close to the language border. Written on the birds. She shuffled dizzily along the branch, defaced on its sign: *ƷOttenburg*.

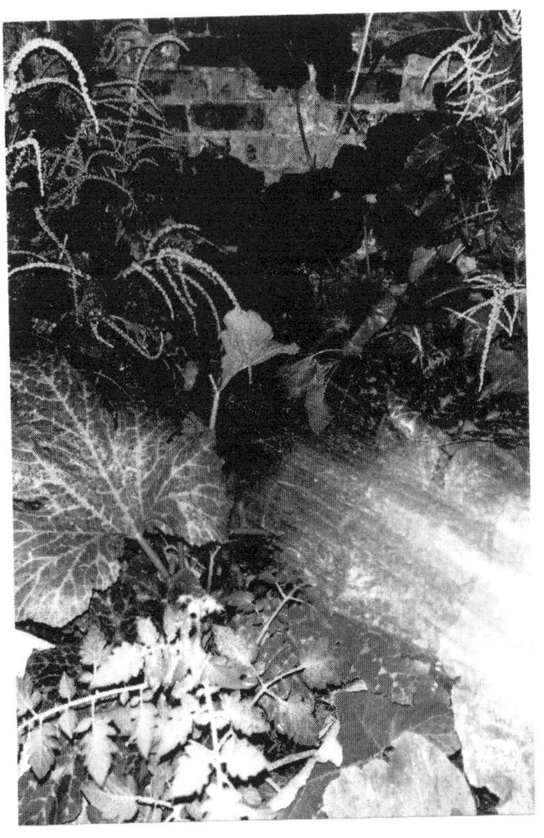

~~piss~~——————————————— ,

, *(notes)*

gliss. notes ^(trans.)

rescue

                      wings

 hoe   hoist

           55

packed,

(as in

  soil or

  snow)

what is kelp?— biggest form of seaweed
(a very general term (like headache vs
migraine)), she grows in rocky coastlines
in saltwater that is nutrient rich, brown,

grows at lowest part of shore, almost
always below water even at low tide—
grows into kelp forests several metres tall.

very beautiful.   they believe the wave to be
                             the wind

Delicious, dangerous approach of noon.
The shadow of the tree is the vertigo of
the naked soul that in itself consults and
decides. These kelp-ways born of the
branch, balancing in the breeze,
misjudging. They think that a wave is the
wind.

Young phantoms, exceeding silence!

surpassing/exceeding
hope/expectations
unexpected

to come to
the wrong
conclusion about
something

accost, dock, land

                          La fin — the end / the ending - not
                          the passing of a 'natural'
                          time, dawn / evening, but
                          the end of the journey, of
he docks/stops   the conquest, of his belief
only for the end   that he can master time,
of his journey   bend it to his will (to fight,
                          claim gold and dominate
                          history — which is man's
                          telling of the past, an
                                  imposition)

           —what's the word for this that's as
           incisive as *la fin* culmination?

                          conflict?
                          fighting?

sea-foamed?

"Time passes, and its passing makes me swell," and he
becomes afraid!…

Glissant's *puis* — time,
consequence the result of a
process, decision or habit,
in reaction to what's inside
(internal judgments) vs listening /
responding to what is outside.

>*triomphes* — triumphs, but another way of winning—
>grasping mistakenly, a win *at cost*

>victory, achievement, gain. a temporal consequence
>but also a subjective one - both for the phenomena the
>poem is encountering, as well as the voice of the poem
>which is witness to the interaction / interplay of these
>systems / environments, but whose voice + thoughts are
>/ have been shaped by them

>—it coagulates around the moment of this
>consequence.

habits / ways / methods / behaviour

Delicious and dangerous approach of noon, casting its vertiginous pride in the shadow of the tree whose bared soul confers and confides in only itself.

What consequences for these misled triumphs? For balancing in the breeze as kelp does which being born of the branch, mistakes the wave for the wind.

Nascent fantasies, unexpected silence!

christopher ~~topher~~ notes ^{*(trans.)*}

      wings   s

                     wings win d ing

                              sss

                                _inside

ssseparate_a ppearssss i gh isss   topher   gho
           pparition   windled

                                sssssst—*!*

                dw——— indle

     dull   idle

        muscled

          & musicless hope

               (o hoper

                            in open

       O—*!*)

small image to *ppphhhh*

                ferry

                      to b ear

                        &

be born —*e*

            across

                                &   between seas

                  breezeborn   *e*

dove   *s*   wing   *s*

        (to cross out

           my names)

...—& notes ,

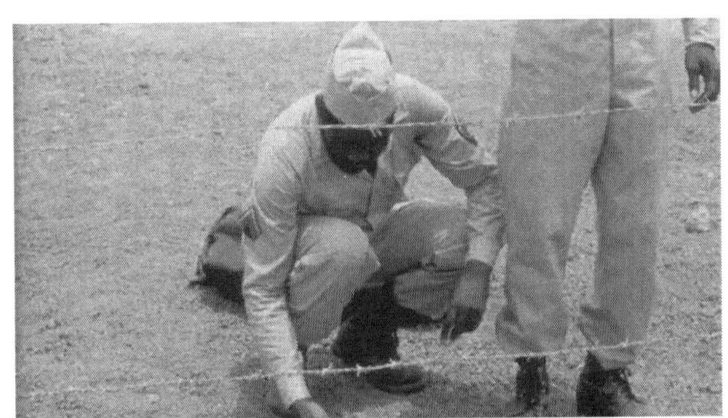

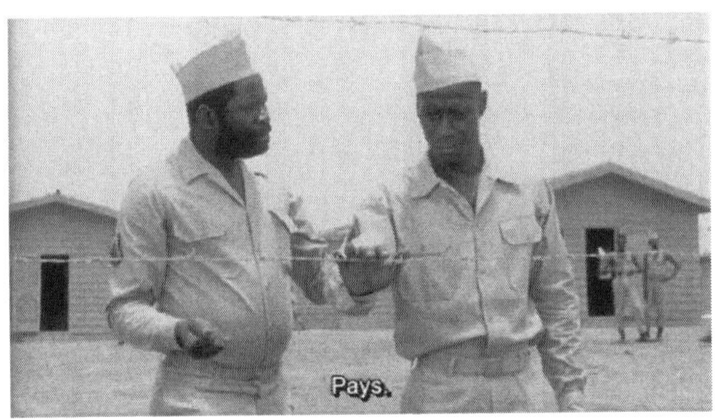

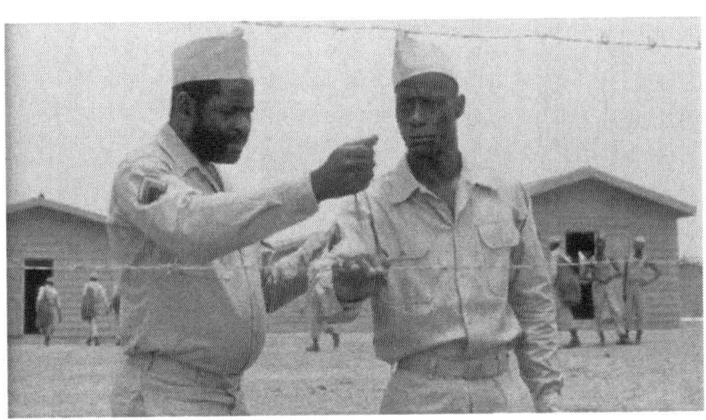

Ousmane Sèmbene, *Campe de Thiaroye*, 1988

From whose perspective are the lips of the African thick or her hair kinky? Certainly not from the African's perspective. And there is no denying that expressions such as "thick lips" and "kinky hair" connote far more than they denote. How then does the writer describe the Caribbean descendants of West Africans so as not to connote the negativity implied in descriptions such as "thick lips?"

Journal entry, Dec. 11, 1986 (Testimony stoops to Mother Tongue)

*I want to write about kinky hair and flat noses —
maybe I should be writing about the language that
kinked the hair and flattened noses, made jaws
prognathous*

M Nourbese Philip, *The Absence of Writing or How I Almost Became a Spy* in *she tries her tongue, her silence softly breaks*, p 86

p 25   *& i fear*

                    all images

I fear all images   might still
conspire, breathe
together   to make a sick
salvific sense into me—

Dan Schapiro, *HOLEPLAY*, p 13

beetroot. It is amazing how this tuber has been an invisible force in the French Carribean. What happened in the foggy plains of Northern France has changed the tropical landscape of Martinique.

*

The Process of Dispossession

Economic Principle	Type of production	Currency	Social Characteristics
barter (1st phase)	unorganised predatory economy (fragmented production)	the pound of sugar as currency	hesitation between "centrifugal" and "centripetal" growth
barter (2nd phase)	predatory economy; plantation system (monoproduction)	"local" currency dependent on "national" currency	massive contribution to the French economy
pseudo-production	pseudoeconomy; declining production artificially maintained (malproduction)	"local" currency absorbed by "national" currency	victory of French beet-sugar farmers
exchange	negated economy; intermittent attempts to rehabilitate (nonproduction)	disappearance of "local" currency	assimilation; exchange of public funds for private benefit and reexport

Edouard Glissant, *Carribean Discourse*, pgs 43 & 157

p 27   *stretch / across the corpus of the group*

But for the most noticeable change the metal industry brought here:

The burials. The word afterlife is unavoidable. Still, inhumed, with a very similar burial procedure to Windmill Hill Neolithic. But it's impossible to see the life once gone belonging as it had to the community. A man's life had become his possession, like his dagger and his bow, and eternally his.

[...] the communal feeling was gone, and a burial system which had served to emphasise a continuity in the corpus of the group emphasised instead the continuity of the individual which only makes sense logically as an afterlife.

Peter Riley, *Working Notes on British Prehistory or Archeological Guesswork One*, in *Certain Prose of the English Intelligencer*, p 63.

p 28   *sorry bramble*

The sky   is a picture of being sorry

Dan Schapiro, *HOLEPLAY*, p 28

p 38   *the cat trees*

T H O U G H T S *HELP* BROKEN
VOICED *HELP* NEEDED **FEET**

TO WALK WITHOUT BREATHING
BUT WHAT ABOUT THE CAT TREES
UP DISORIENTATING *[…]*

Candace Hill, *How To Make* in *Muss Sill*, p 2

p 46   *an access whose meaning she could not escape*

I am not really sure I have anything to say about
area studies—about the maps of the world it created,
about the maps of the world it still uses, about
how it assembles knowledge, about the academy's
complicity in it, about the role of native informants,
about the possibilities of antinomian practices, about
decolonization (a term whose current use in online
communities makes little sense to me), about earnest
US-based scholars who promise not to replicate
imperial strategies as they travel around the world
to discover, if they dare, that they hold US passports,
and this means something they cannot escape. I could
think about what that means for those who travel
with good intentions, but I do not really see the point.

How will the frog choose to die?

Keguro Macharia, *On Being Area-Studied: A Litany of
Complaint*, GLQ: A Journal of Lesbian and Gay Studies,
Volume 22, Number 2, April 2016, p 188

pgs 53-59

transcribed from my notes
made while attempting to translate

Sacre in *La terre inquiète*, and
XXIII in *Les Indes*

both from Edouard Glissant's *Poèmes complets*

thank you,

air / time was broadcast on Plastique Fantastique's *Termite Radio* on Resonance FM Extra, a previous version has been published in *Re.Creation: A Queer Anthology. sorry bramble* was published in *Ludd Gang 12.* thank you to their respective editors and curators.

, &

Bambi, my sister. Shenece, the friend I sit with. Andy, the girl who could tell. Sara and baby Sebastian. Elaine Mitchener, the improviser. Ain Bailey. Danielle, my sister who helped me with the translations into Flemish. Marcus, whose garden I am watering in the picture. the entire and extended Friary Road family. Glyn, Tammy and the cohort. petals, s*an, Dan, Jett, Nat, Jennifer, Alicia, Daniela, Taylor,

Bhanu Kapil, the87press

, &

, all my friends
in these things